# SERIOUSLY

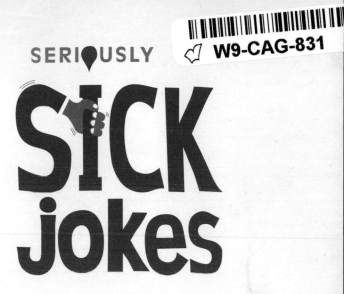

# SICK
# jokes

# SERI●USLY

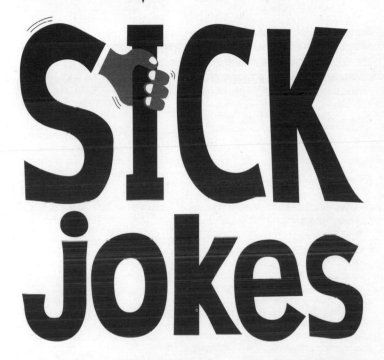

# SiCK Jokes

*The Most Disgusting, Filthy, Offensive Jokes from the Vile, Obscene, Disturbed Minds of b3ta.com*

## Rob Manuel

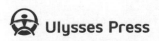 **Ulysses Press**

Published in the United States by
ULYSSES PRESS
P.O. Box 3440
Berkeley, CA 94703
www.ulyssespress.com

First published as *The Bumper B3ta Book of Sick Jokes* in 2006 in the U.K.
by Friday Books

Printed in Canada by Webcom

10 9 8 7 6 5 4 3 2

ISBN13: 978-1-56975-709-3
Library of Congress Control Number: 2008911762

Acquisitions Editor: Nick Denton-Brown
Managing Editor: Claire Chun
Editor: Keith Riegert
Design: what!design @ whatweb.com
Editorial: Lauren Harrison
Production: Abigail Reser

Distributed by Publishers Group West

# Contents

# Introduction

Oh dear God, how are we supposed to introduce this? In your hands, you are holding the most depraved, foul and offensive collection of jokes ever compiled into one book.

You're probably expecting us to write something to justify this collection, aren't you? Something intellectual and wordy that explains how these jokes are actually a reflection of society's pressure points and fears? Nope. Sorry. You'll have to look elsewhere for that stuff because we know the sordid truth: Sick jokes are guilty pleasures. They're pleasures that can be shared when you're sure no easily offended people are listening.

And we've got the whole damn lot of them, even the ones that made censors say, "No, you can't print that! They'll fire-bomb the publishers!" But don't worry. If you do find yourself getting nauseated, just turn to the "panic page" in the back of the book where we've stuck some nice fluffy jokes and a picture of a kitten. See? All better now.

Enjoy the book!

# How This Book Was Made

Every joke in this book was submitted by the public. That's the cunning "get out" clause. This is *your* book! Not ours!

You see, we have a famous website called b3ta.com, and we asked our visitors to send in their sickest jokes. And they did, in hordes. Two-and-a-half thousand of them to be exact, and when we threw away the crappy ones, we were left with this bunch here.

Then we did the clever part: We asked the site readers to send in illustrations to make the book look pretty. There's a full list of credits at the back, so if you want to give these people work, it should be easy enough to find them.

So that was our dream. To make a book simply by asking the Internet to do it for us. And it worked. Lazy jerks? Us? Yep.

# Celebrity and News Events

Whenever there is a news event involving a major disaster or a celebrity, there is always a joke to go with it. And it's either told in a bar, texted on a phone or sent by e-mail. Here are some of your favorites.

**What was the last thing to go through Kurt Cobain's mind as he pulled the trigger?**
A bullet.

**Elton John is getting a divorce.**
He found out his husband was having sex behind his back.

**What's black and shoots across a room?**
Marvin Gaye's dad.

**How does Victoria Beckham screw in a light bulb?**
She holds it in the socket as the world revolves around her.

**What's the difference between a diamond ring and David Beckham?**
Nothing, they both come in a Posh box.

**Why does Mike Tyson cry after sex?**
He's got mace in his eyes.

**Just before leaving for the airport for their fateful flight, JFK Jr.'s wife, Carolyn Bessette Kennedy, asked her husband if they should shower before boarding the airplane.**
He replied, "No, I think we'll just wash up on the beach."

# George Bush dies and is sent to hell.

Satan explains to Bush that hell is overcrowded and that he needs to evict someone else to make room.

*"I'll give you a choice," says Satan, and he shows Bush three rooms.*

In the first room is JFK being stretched on a rack.

*"If you choose this room," says Satan, "you will be tortured on the rack forever."*

*"Don't want that," says Bush, and he is shown the second room.*

Behind the next door is Richard Nixon, who is being ripped apart by rabid baboons.

*"If you choose this room," says Satan, "you will be mutilated by rabid baboons forever."*

*"That's no good either," says Bush, and so Satan opens the final door.*

Bush jumps for joy as he sees Bill Clinton being blown off by Monica Lewinsky—forever.

*"I'll take this one!" says George "This one!" Satan shrugs and says, "Okay Monica, you can go..."*

# Dancing on your ceiling

▶ Ghosts are often claimed to be hallucinations. Certainly people can be tricked into 'seeing' things that do not exist. Stare at the cross in the centre of Lionel Ritchie's face, while you count slowly to 120. Then look at a plain ceiling. You should 'see' a phantom Lionel Ritchie dancing on the ceiling. If the image has not faded within 5 minutes, consult an optomexorcist.

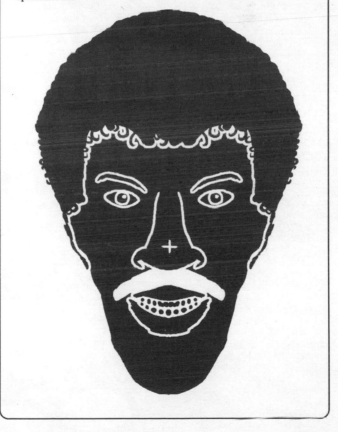

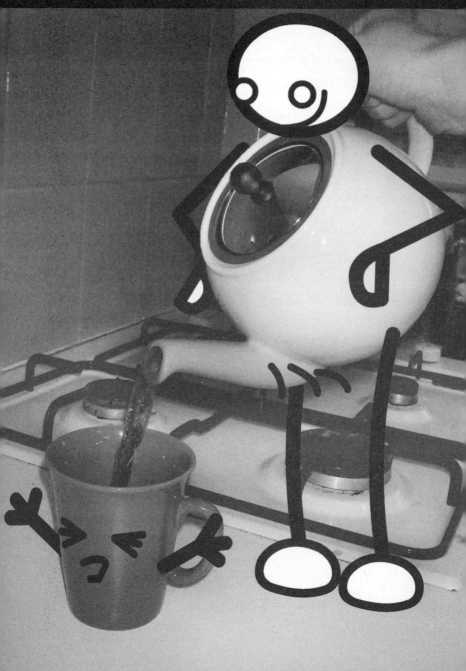

**What's black and slid down Nelson's Column?**
Winnie Mandela.

**What's green and 50 feet tall?**
Nelson Mandela's lawn.

**What's yellow and lives off dead beetles?**
Yoko Ono.

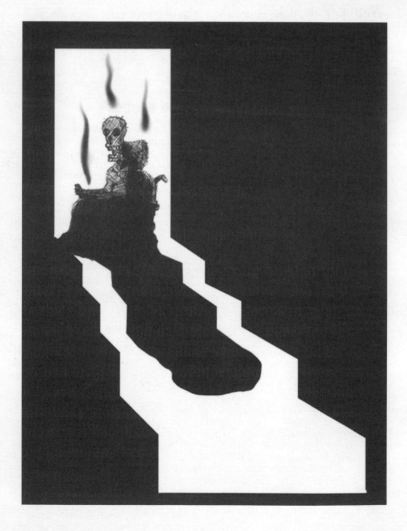

# Christopher Reeve

Oh, the irony: Superman ends up in a wheelchair. Now that he's dead, you may wish to note that Christopher Reeve jokes are interchangeable with Steven Hawking jokes (or any poor guy who ends up in a wheelchair).

**Why didn't Superman stop the World Trade Center attacks?**

Because he's a quadriplegic.

**What's the opposite of Christopher Reeve?**

Christopher Walken.

# Michael Jackson

**What did the woman say to Michael Jackson on the beach?**

"Can you move please? You're in my son."

**What's small, brown and warm, and found in the back of little boys' underwear?**

Michael Jackson's hand.

**What's the difference between Neil Armstrong and Michael Jackson?**

Neil Armstrong was the first man to *walk* on the *moon*, and Michael Jackson enjoys fucking.

**What's the difference between Michael Jackson and a tin can?**

One's used for storing food, the other fucks…

**What do Michael Jackson and shopping bags have in common?**

Both are made of plastic and dangerous to children.

**Did you hear that McDonald's is coming out with a McJackson burger?**

It's a 50-year-old piece of meat in a 12-year-old bun.

**Knock, knock.**
*Who's there?*
**Little Boy Blue.**
*Little Boy Blue who?*
**Michael Jackson.**

**What's 12 inches long and sits on the floor at the foot of Michael Jackson's bed?**

His latest boyfriend's pants.

**What's blond, had six legs and runs through Michael Jackson's dreams?**

Hanson.

**Did you hear about Michael Jackson's latest vacation destination?**

He's going to Tampa with the kids.

**Why does Michael Jackson like sex with 28-year-olds?**

Because there are 20 of them.

**What is the difference between Saddam Hussein and Michael Jackson?**

Saddam didn't enter Jordan.

**What's the difference between Michael Jackson and acne?**

Acne doesn't come on your face until you're 13.

**Michael Jackson's wife has just given birth. He asks the doctor how long it will be before they can have sex.**

The doctor says, "For fuck's sake, Michael, at least wait until it can walk."

**Why did Michael Jackson phone Boyz II Men?**
He thought they were a delivery service.

**What is the worst thing about being Michael Jackson?**
You have to go to bed before 7:00 p.m.

**What's the difference between greyhound racing and Michael Jackson?**
The greyhounds wait for the hare.

**How do you know when it is bedtime at Neverland Ranch?**
When the big hand touches the little hand.

**Michael Jackson is sitting in his living room surfing the Internet on his laptop. All of a sudden, the front door whips open and his girlfriend storms in. She screams, "You fucking asshole!" and heads into the bedroom. Stunned, Michael turns off the computer and walks toward the bedroom, wondering, "Now what have I done?" Inside the bedroom he finds the girl furiously packing a suitcase. He asks her what's up and she responds with a hiss, "My therapist says that I should leave you and that you're a pedophile!"**
Michael responds, "Wow, that's a pretty big word for an eight-year-old."

# Helen Keller

Helen Keller was a deaf and blind woman whose story was told to countless school kids via the tearjerker movie *The Miracle Worker.* We're very sorry to inform you that lots of those kids snickered and made bad jokes about her and then e-mailed them to us. And here they are!

**Did you know that Helen Keller had a tree house?**
Neither did she.

**What did Helen Keller's parents do when she was bad?**
Leave the plunger in the toilet.

**Why does Helen Keller wear tight jeans?**
So people can read her lips.

**What did Helen Keller say when she fell off the cliff?**
Nothing, she had her mittens on.

**Why did Helen Keller drive her car off a cliff?**
Because she's a woman.

**Why did Helen Keller masturbate with one hand?**
So she could moan with the other.

**What did Helen Keller call her kids?**
Muuurrghhrrhurrg.

# Stevie Wonder

Did you know that Stevie was blind? Ah, yes. We know that this is a shocking revelation, but please bear with us, there is a reason that we are telling you: People can use this fact to make jokes. Actually, many of these jokes can be rewritten for the famous blind people du jour: Ray Charles, David Blunkett and…um…many others too.

**Why is Stevie Wonder always smiling?**
He doesn't know he's black.

**How did Stevie Wonder burn his ear?**
The phone rang and he answered the iron.

**How did Stevie Wonder burn his other ear?**
The person called back.

**What's black and loud?**
Stevie Wonder answering the iron.

**You ever seen Stevie Wonder's wife?**
Neither has he.

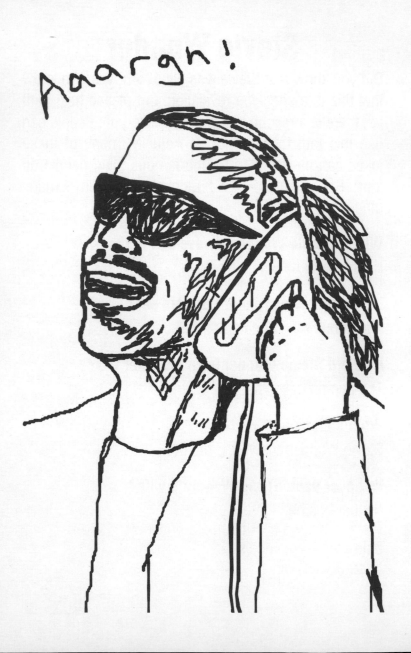

Stevie Wonder is playing his first gig in Tokyo, and the place is absolutely packed to the rafters. In an attempt to break the ice with his new audience, he asks if anyone would like him to play a request. A little old Japanese man jumps out of his seat in the first row and shouts at the top of his lungs, "Play a jazz chord! Play a jazz chord!" Amazed that this guy knows about the jazz influences in Stevie's varied career, the blind impresario starts to play an E-minor scale and then goes into a difficult jazz melody for about ten minutes. When he finishes, the whole place goes wild. The little old man jumps up again and shouts, "No, no, play a jazz chord, play a jazz chord." A bit ticked off by this, Stevie, being the professional that he is, dives straight into a jazz improvisation on the B-flat minor scale with his band and really tears the place apart. The crowd goes wild with this impromptu show of his technical expertise. The little old man jumps up again and says, "No, no. Play a jazz chord, play a jazz chord." Outraged that this little guy doesn't seem to appreciate his playing ability, Stevie says to him from the stage, "Okay, smart ass. You get up here and do it!"

The little old man climbs up on the stage, takes hold of the mike and starts to sing "A jazz chord to say I ruv you..."

**What does Stevie Wonder's wife do when they've had a fight?**
She rearranges the furniture.

**What goes "Click…click…Is that it? Click…click…Is that it? Click…click…Is that it?"**
Stevie Wonder doing a Rubik's Cube.

**What's the fastest thing on land?**
Stevie Wonder's speed boat.

**What's Stevie Wonder's favorite color?**
Corduroy.

**Why can't Stevie Wonder read?**
Because he's black.

**Stevie Wonder was in a horrendous car accident the other week.**
His life flashed before his ears.

**Endless love: Stevie Wonder and Ray Charles playing tennis.**

# Princess Diana

**Why was Princess Diana drunk on the night of the crash?**

She had a couple of pints of Carling in her.

**Why did Princess Diana have a Mercedes?**

She wouldn't be seen dead in a Honda.

**Why did Elton John sing at Princess Diana's funeral?**

Because he was the only queen who gave a fuck.

**...and remember, there's always light at the end of the tunnel...
unless you're Princess Diana.**

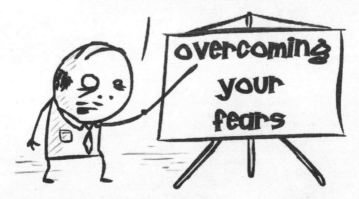

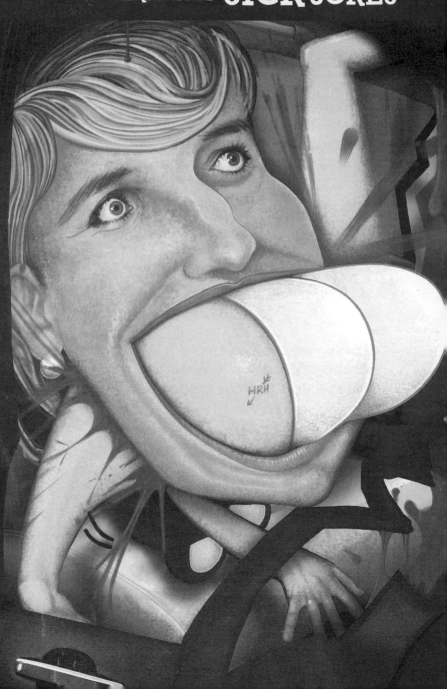

**What's the difference between Princess Diana and Michael Hutchence?**

Michael Hutchence was wearing his belt.

**What do Princess Diana and Ferrero Rocher chocolates have in common?**

They both come out of France in a fancy box.

**Why did Princess Diana cross the road?**

She wasn't wearing her seat belt.

**What do Princess Diana and Pink Floyd have in common?**

Their last big hit was *The Wall*.

**How did they know Princess Diana had dandruff?**

They found her Head and Shoulders in the glove compartment.

**Did you know that Princess Diana was on the phone when she crashed?**

She was also on the dashboard, the windshield, the gearshift and the headrest.

**What would Princess Diana be doing now if she were still alive?**

Scratching the shit out of the lid of her coffin.

**What's the difference between a Mercedes and Princess Diana?**

A Mercedes will reach 40.

**What did Princess Diana do when she heard the driver had been drinking?**

She hit the roof.

**What's the one word that could have saved Princess Diana's life?**

"Taxi."

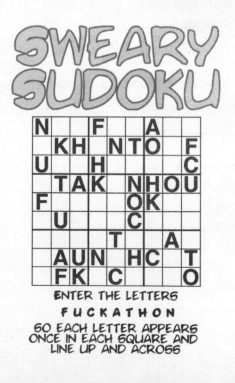

ENTER THE LETTERS

**F U C K A T H O N**

SO EACH LETTER APPEARS
ONCE IN EACH SQUARE AND
LINE UP AND ACROSS

**What's the difference between Mother Teresa and Princess Diana?**
About five days.

**What were Princess Diana's last words?**
"Have you been dri–"

# Space Shuttle

There have been two space shuttle disasters, *Challenger* in 1986 and *Columbia* in 2003. We are pretty sure that you can reuse these jokes if there is a third disaster in 2020.

**What's the last recorded message on the space shuttle's black box?**
"Go ahead, let the woman drive."

**What's NASA's official drink?**
7UP on the rocks with a splash of teachers.

**Why does NASA drink Sprite?**
Because they can't get 7UP.

**What does NASA stand for?**
Need Another Seven Astronauts.

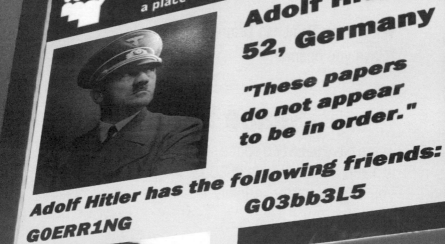

# Hitler

There's just something about Adolf that's funny. We think it has something to do with school history lessons, when you had to take it all so seriously. Or maybe it's just the moustache. Either way, doing a quick Hitler impression always gets a laugh even if you're a crappy comedian. And if you're reading this Freddie Starr, yes, we mean you.

**Knock, knock.**
*Who's there?*
**Guess.**
*Guess who?*
**The Gestapo, Miss Frank. Now open ze door!**

**Knock, knock.**
*Who's there?*
**Gestapo.**
*Gestapo who?*
**VE ASK ZE KVESTIONS! [Slap]**

**How do you crucify a spastic?**
On a swastika.

**Why do German men grow moustaches?**
So they can look like their mothers.

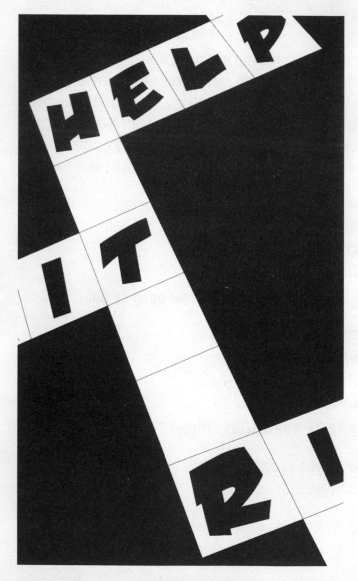

**Crossword clue: 5 down, Jewish baker**

**What's brown and hides in the attic?**
The diarrhea of Anne Frank.

**Why did Hitler commit suicide?**
He saw the gas bill.

**My Grandad died in a concentration camp.**
  *Really?*
**Yeah, he fell out of his machine-gun tower.**

**I'll never forgive the Germans for the way they treated my grandpa during the war; passed over for promotion, time and time again.**

**What do you do with a Jew with ADD?**
Put him in a concentration camp.

**Hitler walks into the meeting room, turns to his trusted staff and says, "I want you to organize the execution of 10,000 Jews and two hedgehogs." Everyone looks around the table, and after a long silence, Goering pipes up, "Mein Führer, why do you want to kill two hedgehogs?"**
Hitler smiles, turns to the rest of the table and says, "You see, no one cares about the Jews."

**Three Jews win the lottery and collect the $8 million jackpot. They are getting ready to divvy up the cash, and one says, "Right, so that's $2 million to me, $2 million to each of you and $2 million to the Germans." The other two reply, "$2 million to the fucking GERMANS? What the fuck for?"**

Says the first Jew, rolling up his sleeve, "Well, they did give us the numbers."

**How many Jews can you fit in a sedan?**

Five in the seats and about a million in the ashtray.

# Sex and Love

▾   ▾   ▾

What is funnier than sex? Awkward, perverted sex! Possibly involving your mother, other loved ones or dead people.

**Why does Dr. Pepper come in a bottle?**
Because his wife is dead.

**Did you hear about the man with five penises?**
His pants fit like a glove.

**Had my first blow job today...Five whiskeys and I still can't get rid of the taste.**

**What's blue and sticky?**
Smurf cum.

**Why did the condom fly across the room?**
Because it was pissed off.

**Why is porn exactly like a real relationship?**
It doesn't cuddle you afterward, give you a pet name or care about you.

**What's blue and comes in Brownies?**
Cub Scouts.

**Down the street lives a family of prostitutes. The daughter charges $20 for a blow job, the mother charges $5, and the granny is just pleased to get a warm drink.**

**What's the difference between a drug dealer and a hooker?**

A hooker can wash her crack and sell it again.

**How does a cheap hooker turn the light on after sex?**

She opens the car door.

**What's the difference between a family reunion and doing 69?**

In 69 you only have to kiss one cunt.

**Ever tried Belgian kissing? It's like French kissing, but with more Flem.**

**What did the cannibal do after he dumped his girlfriend?**

Wiped his ass.

**What do you do with 365 used condoms?**

Melt them down, make a tire and call it a Good Year.

**I took a Viagra the other day and it got stuck in my throat. I've been walking round with a stiff neck ever since.**

**What does 80-year-old pussy taste like?**

Depends.

One sperm says to another, "How long till we reach the egg?" The other sperm replies, "A long way yet, we've only just passed the tonsils."

**What is the loudest sound you'll hear from an 80-year-old during sex?**
The sound of her hips breaking.

**How do you know if you have a very high sperm count?**
Your girlfriend has to chew before she can swallow.

**What's the difference between lust, love and showing off?**
Spitting, swallowing and gargling.

A lonely rich widow puts out a personal ad that says, "Lovely gentleman wanted to share life, love and fortune with. Conditions: 1) Won't beat me up. 2) Won't run away. 3) Good in bed." Predictably, she gets hundreds of offers, but none are suitable. Eventually she answers her doorbell and sees a man with no arms and no legs.

*"Who are you?" she asks.*

*"I'm your dream husband!" he replies. "I've got no arms, so I can't beat you up, and I've got no legs, so I can't run away."*

*"Are you good in bed?"*

*"I rang the doorbell, didn't I?"*

**What did Cinderella do when she got to the ball?**
She choked.

**What do a pussy and a grape have in common?**
The best ones squirt when you eat them.

**What's green and yellow and eats nuts?**
Gonorrhea.

**A man says to the doctor, "I've been raped by an elephant!" The doctor examines the man's butt and says, "You're right. But your hole is ten inches wide. An elephant's member is only two inches wide. How'd it get that big?"**

*"He fingered me first."*

**What is the difference between a dog and a fox?**
About five drinks.

# Incest

Oh, and a bit of necrophilia for kicks.

**I said to my sister, "You're a better fuck than Mom."**
She replied "Yeah, Dad said the same thing."

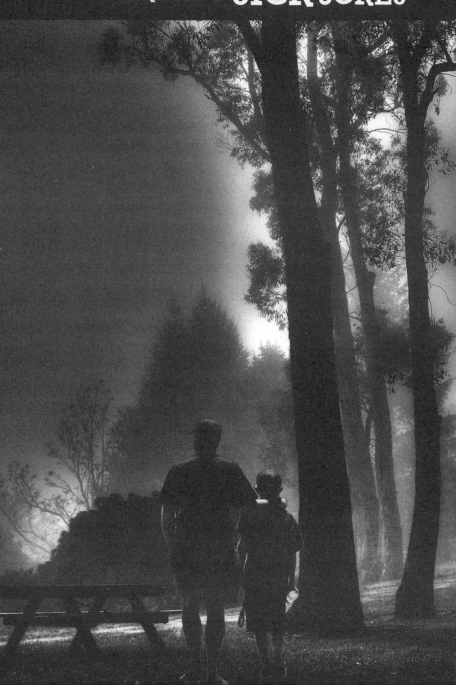

**What's the difference between your mom, your sister and your girlfriend?**
I haven't fucked your sister.

**What's sicker than fingering your three-year-old sister?**
Finding your old man's wedding ring while you're up there.

**It's not rape if they're dead.**

**I used to be a necrophiliac...but the rotten cunt split on me.**

**Necrophilia: Crack open a cold one!**

# More Pedophiles

If you weren't fed up with molestation jokes already, here are some more. Kids love 'em.

**How do you know if a Catholic priest is a pedophile?**
Ask him two questions: Are you Catholic? Are you a priest?

**Did you hear about the reverse exorcism?**
The devil couldn't get the priest out of the boy.

**What do you call a pedophile pirate?**
Yarr Kelly.

**What's the benefit of having sex with 28-year-olds?**
There are twenty of them.

**What's the benefit of having sex with 91-year-olds?**
Experience.

## A father is in the bathtub with his three-year-old son.

*Child: Daddy, why is my peepee different from yours?*

*Father: Well Son, for a start, yours isn't erect.*

A guy goes to the pharmacy and says, "I need some condoms for my 11-year-old daughter." The pharmacist is shocked and asks, "Your daughter is sexually active at 11?" The guy says, "Not really, she just lies there like her little brother."

I like my whisky like I like my women: Eight-years-old and mixed with coke.

A man pulls up in his car beside a little boy. He opens the door, holds out a brown paper bag of candy and says, "Hey kid, if I give you a candy, will you come in my car?" The kid replies, "Gimme the bag and I'll come in your mouth."

What do you do after having a baby?

Put its diaper back on.

What's cracked when you fuck it and fucked when you crack it?

A baby's pelvis.

**What did the Jewish pedophile say to the little boy once he was in the car?**

"Hey, go easy on the candy, I'm not made of money!"

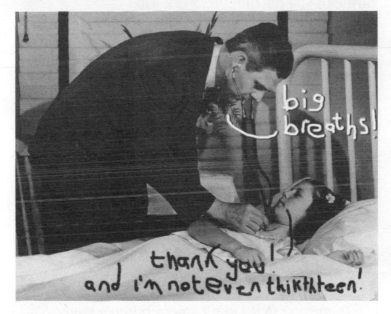

**What's black and blue and afraid of sex?**

The eight-year-old in my basement.

**What kind of file do you need to turn a half-inch hole into a two-inch hole?**

A pedophile.

What do you call a toddler with a runny nose?
Full.

How can you tell that there are two
elephants in your fridge?
You have to put the half-eaten dismembered body
parts of your infant daughter in the freezer instead.

## Katie is five-years-old.
## Tomorrow is her birthday.

*"Dad, guess how old I'll be tomorrow?"
she asks.*

*"Don't know," he replies.*

*"I'll be six!" she exclaims.*

She goes into the kitchen and sees her grandad.

*"Grandad, guess how old I'll be tomorrow?"*

*"To answer that I need you to remove your
panties," he says.*

So she does and he sniffs them. Then he fingers her,
smells his finger and licks it.

*"You will be six tomorrow," he says.*

*"How do you know that?" she asks.*

*"I heard you talking to your dad."*

**A pedophile goes for a walk and sees a little girl crying by the edge of a cliff.**

*He says, "Little girl, why are you crying?"*

*She says, "I just got out of the car to pee and the car rolled off the cliff and my whole family was in it. Now they're all dead!"*

*"Well," says the pedophile, unzipping his fly, "it's not your lucky day, is it?"*

# Scatological

Our jokes are shit. Literally. (Did you see what we did there? Did you?)

**Why did the baker have smelly hands?**
Because he kneaded a poo.

*Little boy: Mommy, Mommy, can I lick the bowl clean?*

*Mother: No, just flush it like everyone else does.*

**What's the difference between a rectal thermometer and an oral thermometer?**
The taste.

**A teacher is reading a story to her class of toddlers when she notices a wet patch all around a little girl.**

*Teacher: Oh, Katie, why didn't you put your hand up?*

*Katie: I did! But it trickled through my fingers.*

**Four men are arguing about what the fastest thing in the world is.**

*Man #1 says, "It's thought: You think about moving and you move."*

*Man #2 says, "No, it's blinking: You do it all the time and don't realize."*

*Man #3 says, "Electricity: You flip a switch and hundreds of miles away a light turns on right away."*

*Man #4 says, "All wrong, it's diarrhea: I needed the toilet and before I could think, blink or turn on the light, I'd shit myself!"*

**How did the constipated mathematician relieve himself?**

He worked it out with a pencil.

# Misogyny

Ooh, look! We've used a complicated word for "sexism." Check out us and our fantastic vocabulary. BTW: Our favorite sexist lyric is Kool G's "Chicks are on my dick like a human shish kebab." Nice work if you can get it.

**How do you get a fat girl into bed?**
Piece of cake.

**What do you call a 300-pound woman?**
Fat.

**I like my women the way I like my coffee: ground up and in my freezer.**

**Why do men fart more than women?**
Because women can't shut up long enough to build up the required pressure.

**What's it called when a woman is paralyzed from the waist down?**
Marriage.

**Why are women like washing machines?**
They both leak when they're fucked.

**Why do women have legs?**
Have you seen the mess snails make?

**A man is in a bar and spots a gorgeous girl.
He walks over to her and says, "Know the
difference between a Big Mac and a blow job?"**

*"No," she replies.*

*"Wanna go for lunch?"*

**An undertaker says to a bereaved husband,
"When did you realize your wife was dead?"**

*"Well," he replies, "the sex was the same
but the dishes just kept piling up."*

**How many men does it take to fix a vacuum cleaner?**
Why the fuck should we fix it? We never use it!

**There are a half-million women in the world
battered daily, and all this time I've been eating
mine plain.**

**What's the difference between a bucket of sand
and a bucket menstrual blood?**
You can't gargle sand.

**Why does a woman have a forehead?**
So you have somewhere to kiss her after the blow job.

**What's the big fleshy thing around the vagina called?**
The woman.

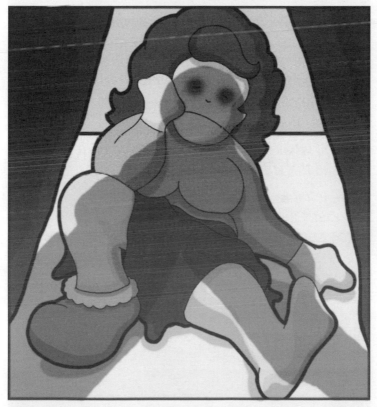

"WHAT DO YOU SAY TO A WOMAN
WITH TWO BLACK EYES?"

"NOTHING, YOU'VE ALREADY
TOLD HER TWICE."

**A man walks into his house after a night at the bar and gives a box to his wife.**

She opens the box and there's a huge frog inside.

*"What's this?" she asks.*

*"That," says her husband "is a wide-mouthed frog. I just bought it from a guy in the bar who had trained it from birth to give the best blow jobs a man could ever wish for. I tried it out on the way home, and its true—it gave the best blow job I've ever had."*

*"Well what do you expect me to do with it?" asks the wife.*

*"Teach it to cook, and then fuck off!"*

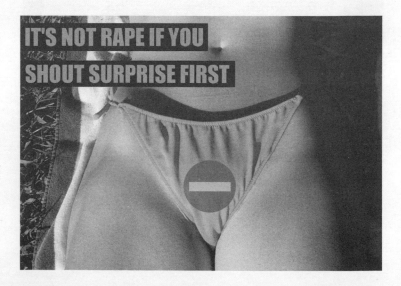

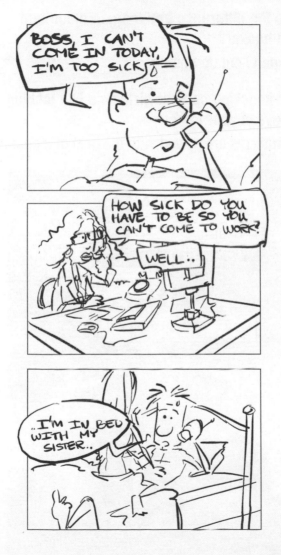

**What's the difference between an onion and a dead hooker?**

I cry when I cut up onions.

**How is knocking up your girlfriend like locking your keys in your car?**

Both problems are solved with the help of a coat hanger.

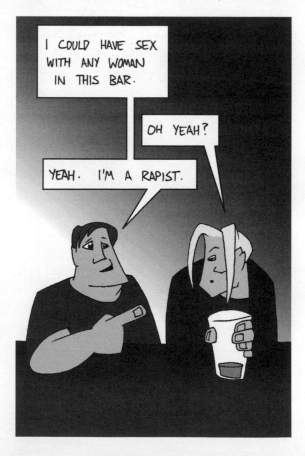

**What has eight legs and makes women scream?**
Gang rape.

**What's black and eats cunt?**
Cervical cancer.

**If a motorcyclist runs over a woman, who's to blame?**
The motorcyclist. He shouldn't have been riding around in the kitchen.

**What do you call an upside-down blonde?**
A brunette with bad breath.

## A blonde is working as hotel maid cleaning rooms.

**One morning she's shocked to find a used condom in a wastebasket.**

*"What?" another maid asked.*
*"Haven't you ever had sex before?"*

*"Yes," the blonde replied,*
*"but never so hard it took the skin off!"*

**Why don't guys like to perform oral sex on a woman the morning after sex?**
Have you ever tried pulling apart a grilled cheese sandwich?

**What do you call a supermodel with a yeast infection?**
Quarter pounder with cheese.

**When I first started dating my new girlfriend, she admitted to me that she had anorexia. These days, it's not going so well. I'm starting to see less and less of her.**

**How many women does it take to decorate a room?**
Depends how thinly you slice them.

**What do you do when the dishwasher stops working?**
Smack her across the face.

**What's the difference between a washing machine and a 15-year-old girl?**
The washing machine won't follow you around for two weeks after you drop a load in it.

**A woman is at work and a man walks up to her and says her hair smells nice. Right away she walks over to an executive and says she wants to file a sexual harassment claim.**

*"What's wrong with someone saying your hair smells nice?" the executive asks.*

*She replies, "He's a midget."*

**What's the smartest thing to ever come out of a woman's mouth?**

Einstein's cock.

**How many feminists does it take to change a light bulb?**

Two: one to change the light bulb, the other to suck my cock.

**Whey do women wear makeup and perfume?**

Because they're ugly and they smell.

**What do you call a Serbian prostitute?**

Slobberdownmycockyoubitch.

**What's the best thing about kinky sex?**

Wiping the blood off the hammer.

**What's the best thing about sex with a dead hooker?**

You don't have to pay her.

**What's the difference between a woman and a computer?**

You only have to punch the information into a computer once.

**What's the first thing a beaten wife should do after coming back from the hospital after the last "incident"?**

The dishes if she knows what's good for her.

**How do you make your girlfriend scream while having sex?**

Call her and tell her.

**What do you call a lesbian with long fingernails?**

Single.

## A man walks into an elevator, which already has a very attractive woman in it.

*As the elevator is going up, he asks, "Excuse me miss, can I smell your pussy?"*

*"Certainly not!" she replies, astonished.*

*"Ah!" he says. "Then it must be your feet."*

**Why does Miss Piggy douche with sugar and vinegar?**

Because Kermit's favorite food is sweet-and-sour pork.

*God: Should I give women legs? Or should I not bother?*

*Angel: Probably, remember the mess that slugs make.*

**What do you call ten vaginas stacked up on top of each other?**

A block of flaps.

# Menstruation

**Fact: Men are scared of women's parts.**
**Fact: Men make jokes about it to cover their fear.**
**Fact: Women know this and find it pathetic.**

**What did one lesbian vampire say to the other?**
See you next month.

**What's the difference between a French woman and a basketball team?**
The basketball team showers after four periods.

**Why do they call it premenstrual syndrome?**
Because mad cow disease was already taken.

**How can you tell if you're dating a tough chick?**
She rolls her own tampons.

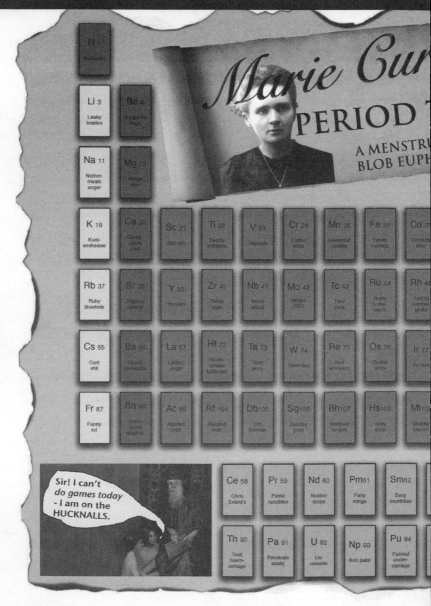

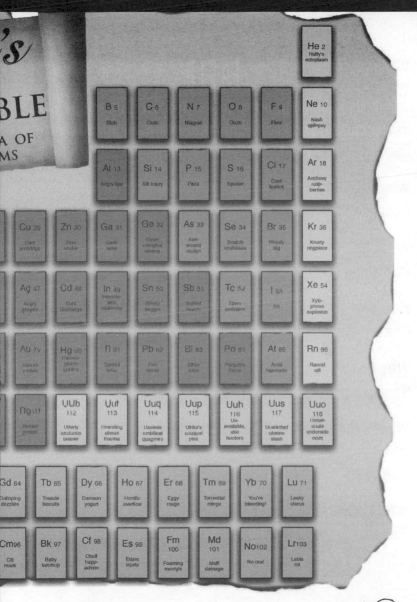

He 2
Huffy's ectoplasm

B 5
Blob

C 6
Clots

N 7
Niagras

O 8
Ooze

F 9
Flow

Ne 10
Nash epilepsy

Al 13
Angry lips

Si 14
Slit injury

P 15
Pain

S 16
Sputter

Cl 17
Cunt lipstick

Ar 18
Anchovy raspberries

Cu 29
Cunt umbridge

Zn 30
Zero nookie

Ga 31
Gash ache

Ge 32
Gynecological enema

As 33
Axe-wound sludge

Se 34
Snatch enchilada

Br 35
Bloody rag

Kr 36
Krusty ringpiece

Ag 47
Angry grower

Cd 48
Cunt discharge

In 49
Intermittent rudeness

Sn 50
Sticky noggin

Sb 51
Stifled beaver

Tc 52
Twat emission

I 53
Ick

Xe 54
Xylophone explosion

Au 79
Autumn undies

Hg 80
Haemoglobin entrails

Tl 81
Tainted lotus

Pb 82
Piss blast

Bi 83
Bitter lotion

Po 84
Parigon's ooze

At 85
Acrid tapenade

Rn 86
Rancid riff

Ng 111
Russet gusset

UUb 112
Utterly unclucous beaver

Uut 113
Unending uterus trauma

Uuq 114
Useless umbilical quagmire

Uup 115
Urlika's unusual piss

Uuh 116
Unavailable, use hooters

Uus 117
Unwanted uterine slush

Uuo 118
Unfortunate underside ooze

Gd 64
Galloping drizzlies

Tb 65
Treacle biscuits

Dy 66
Damson yogurt

Ho 67
Horrific overflow

Er 68
Eggy rouge

Tm 69
Torrential minge

Yb 70
You're bleeding!

Lu 71
Leaky uterus

Cm 96
Clit muck

Bk 97
Baby ketchup

Cf 98
Chuff trappachino

Es 99
Edam squirts

Fm 100
Foaming montyis

Md 101
Muff damage

No 102
No oral

Lr 103
Labia rot

**Why don't midgets use tampons?**
They keep tripping on the string.

**Why do elephants have trunks?**
Because sheep don't have string.

**Why do women have periods?**
Because they fucking deserve them!

**What has two legs and bleeds?**
Half a dog.

**How can you tell the bartender doesn't like you?**
She left the string in your bloody mary.

**Why do tampons have strings?**
So you can floss after you eat.

**What's the difference between a pit bull
and a woman with PMS?**
Lipgloss.

**How did the Red Sea get its name?**
Cleopatra used to bathe there periodically.

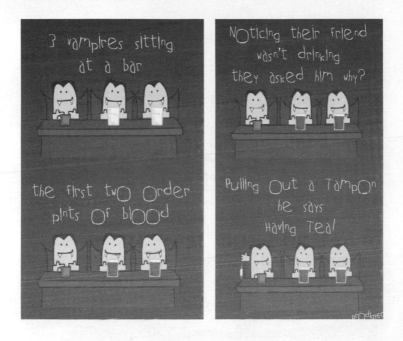

# Anti-men

Anyone who says they hate men just needs to have a chat with a big hard cock.

**Thirty-five-year old women think about having children. What do 35-year old men think about?**

Fucking children.

**Why do you call skin on the end of a cock?**

A man.

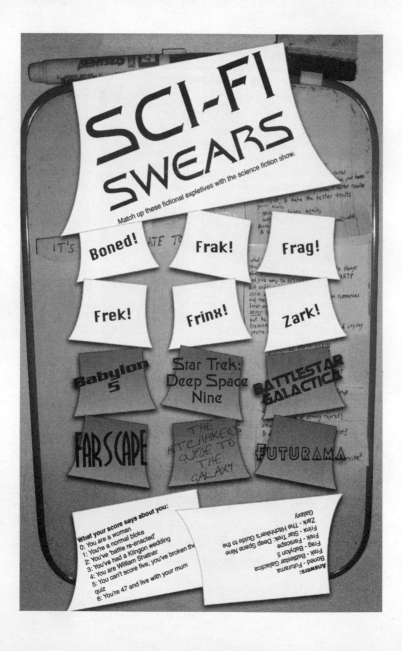

**Why do men have holes in their cocks?**
To stay open minded.

**What did God say after creating man?**
"I can do better."

**How do you scare a man?**
Sneak up behind him and start throwing rice.

**Why is it so hard for women to find men
who are sensitive, caring and good-looking?**
Because they already have boyfriends!

**How do you get a man to do sit-ups?**
Glue the TV remote between his ankles.

**How do you know when a man is getting old?**
He starts having dry dreams and wet farts.

**Why do black widow spiders kill their mates
after sex?**
To stop the snoring before it starts.

**How was Colonel Sanders a typical male?**
All he cared about was legs, breasts and thighs.

**What makes men chase women they have no intention of marrying?**
The same urge that makes dogs chase cars they have no intention of driving.

**What do men have in common with toilet bowls, anniversaries and clitorises?**
They miss them all.

**What do you have when you have two little balls in your hand?**
A man's undivided attention.

**How is a man like a snowstorm?**
You don't know when he's coming, how many any inches you'll get or how long he'll stay.

**What do you call a man with half a brain?**
Gifted.

*Husband: "Want a quickie?"*

*Wife: "As opposed to what?"*

**Why do men find it difficult to make eye contact?**
Breasts don't have eyes.

**Why do men want to marry virgins?**
They can't stand criticism.

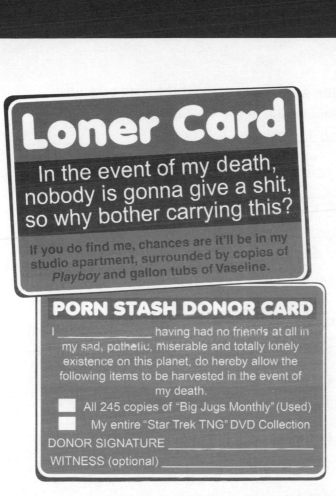

**Loner Card**

In the event of my death, nobody is gonna give a shit, so why bother carrying this?

If you do find me, chances are it'll be in my studio apartment, surrounded by copies of *Playboy* and gallon tubs of Vaseline.

**PORN STASH DONOR CARD**

I _____ having had no friends at all in my sad, pathetic, miserable and totally lonely existence on this planet, do hereby allow the following items to be harvested in the event of my death.

☐ All 245 copies of "Big Jugs Monthly" (Used)
☐ My entire "Star Trek TNG" DVD Collection

DONOR SIGNATURE _____

WITNESS (optional) _____

I went to the state fair and they had one of those "Believe It or Not?" shows. It had a man born with a penis and a brain.

**Why do men name their penises?**

Because they want to be on a first-name basis with the person who makes all their decisions.

**Did you hear the one about the man who won the gold medal at the Olympics?**
He had it bronzed.

**Why do men like masturbation?**
It's sex with someone they love.

*Husband: I don't know why you wear a bra, you don't have anything to put in it.*

*Wife: You wear briefs don't you?*

**What's gross stupidity?**
144 men in one room.

**Why did God create man?**
Because a vibrator can't mow the lawn.

**Why is an impotent man like a Christmas tree?**
They both have balls for decoration.

**Why don't women blink during foreplay?**
They don't have the time.

**Why does it take one million sperm to fertilize one egg?**
They won't stop for directions.

**What do electric toy trains and breasts have in common?**

They're intended for the children, but it's the men who end up playing with them.

**What do men and sperm have in common?**

They both have a one-in-a-million chance of becoming a human being.

# Circumcision

**What does a qualified circumciser get?**

A good tip.

**What does an unqualified circumciser get?**

The sack.

**Circumcision: The pay isn't good, but you can keep the tips**

# Gay

There's a theory that homophobia comes from men who can't accept that they are subconsciously attracted to other men. Who cares! Homophobia is funny. Argh! Does that make us gay? Fantastic, then we can make gay jokes with impunity!

**What's the first symptom of AIDS?**
A sharp, stabbing pain in the rectum.

**How do you know if your best friend is gay?**
He gets a hard-on when you fuck him up the ass.

**How many homosexuals does it take to screw in a light bulb?**
Only one, but it takes an entire emergency room to get it out.

**What's the difference between a gay and a fridge?**
A fridge doesn't fart when you pull your meat out.

**How do you know if you're at a gay picnic?**
The hot dogs all taste like shit.

**Three gay guys were sitting in a hot tub when a blob of semen floated to the surface.**
*"Who farted?"*

**How do you get a gay man to shag your girlfriend?**
Shit in her cunt.

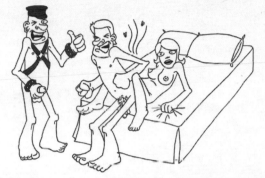

**What did one homosexual in a bar say to the other?**
Pardon me, but can I push in your stool?

**How do you get four homosexuals on a barstool?**
Turn it upside down.

**What did one lesbian frog say to the other
lesbian frog?**
They're right, we DO taste like chicken!

**Now that gay marriage has become legal in many
states, IKEA has responded by exclusively releasing
a new range of lesbian furniture. There's no
screwing involved, and it's all tongue and groove.**

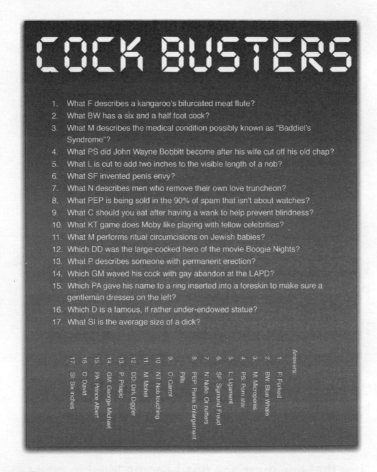

# COCK BUSTERS

1. What F describes a kangaroo's bifurcated meat flute?
2. What BW has a six and a half foot cock?
3. What M describes the medical condition possibly known as "Baddiel's Syndrome"?
4. What PS did John Wayne Bobbitt become after his wife cut off his old chap?
5. What L is cut to add two inches to the visible length of a nob?
6. What SF invented penis envy?
7. What N describes men who remove their own love truncheon?
8. What PEP is being sold in the 90% of spam that isn't about watches?
9. What C should you eat after having a wank to help prevent blindness?
10. What KT game does Moby like playing with fellow celebrities?
11. What M performs ritual circumcisions on Jewish babies?
12. Which DD was the large-cocked hero of the movie Boogie Nights?
13. What P describes someone with permanent erection?
14. Which GM waved his cock with gay abandon at the LAPD?
15. Which PA gave his name to a ring inserted into a foreskin to make sure a gentleman dresses on the left?
16. Which D is a famous, if rather under-endowed statue?
17. What SI is the average size of a dick?

Answers:
1. F: Forked
2. BW: Blue Whale
3. M: Micropenis
4. PS: Porn star
5. L: Ligament
6. SF: Sigmund Freud
7. N: Nutto, Or nutters
8. PEP: Penis Enlargement Pills
9. C: Carrot
10. NT: Nob touching
11. M: Mohel
12. DD: Dirk Diggler
13. P: Priapic
14. GM: George Michael
15. PA: Prince Albert
16. D: David
17. SI: Six inches

**What do you call a lesbian with large fingers?**
Well-hung.

**What do you call a group of lesbians in a field of dildos?**
Squatters.

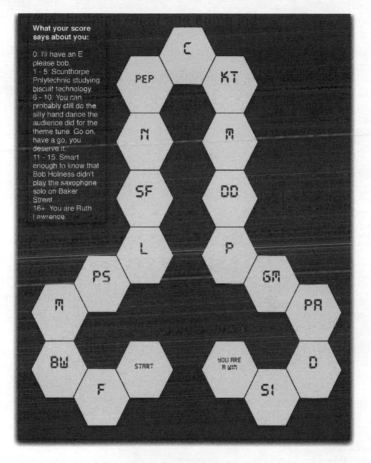

## What do you call an Irish lesbian?

Gaelic.

## What is the hardest thing about rollerblading?

Telling your parents you're gay.

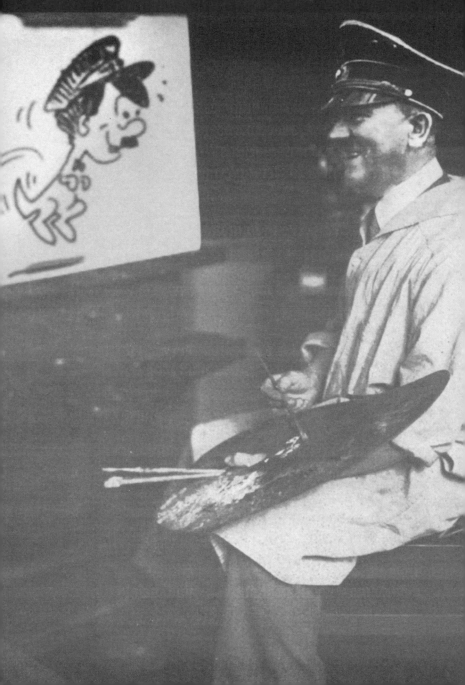

# Religion and Racism

. . .

Because there's nobody who punches up a joke like G.O.D.

# Jewish

We never understood why Hitler gassed the Jews. Jews are useful, unlike the French. He should have gassed the French.

**How do you know if you're in a Jewish household?**
There's a fork in the sugar bowl.

**Why do Jews have big noses?**
Air is free.

**Why do Jews have double-pane windows?**
So their kids can't hear the ice cream truck.

**What happens when a Jew with an erection walks into a wall?**
He breaks his nose.

**What's the difference between a Jew and a canoe?**
A canoe tips.

**What's the definition of a queer Jew?**
Someone who likes girls more than money.

**What's a Jew's worst nightmare?**
Free pork.

# Christian

Seeing as we're taking shots at the Jews and Muslims, it's only fair to take a pop at the God-squad. We're equal opportunity bigots, you see.

**Why is the Bible like a penis?**
You get it forced down your throat by a priest.

**Why can't Jesus eat M&M's?**
He has holes in his hands.

**How can you tell Jesus is coming?**
He's jerking through the hole in his hand.

**What's the difference between Jesus and a picture of Jesus?**
It only takes one nail to hang a picture.

**How do you get a nun pregnant?**
Rape her.

**What's black and white and tells the Pope to fuck off?**
A nun who's won the lottery.

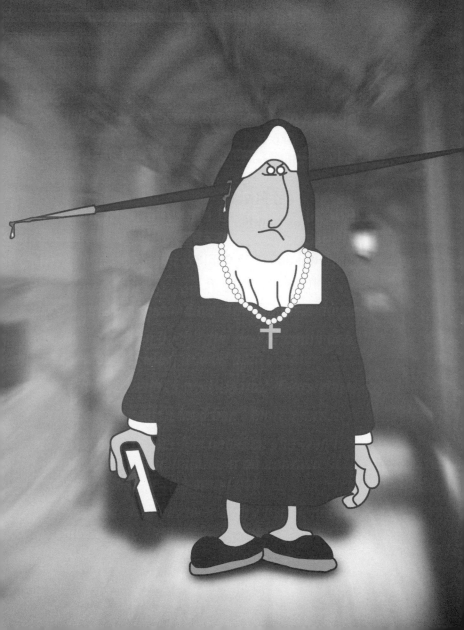

# Muslim

Oh, Muhammad, here we go...

**Two Muslim extremists walk into a bar.**
Boom! Boom!

**A man walks into a sex shop and tells the woman behind the counter that he's looking for a blow-up doll.**

*The woman asks, "Would you like a Christian doll or a Muslim doll?"*

*Confused, the man says, "What's the difference?"*

*"Well," replies the woman, "the Muslim one blows itself up."*

# Buddhism

Are Buddhists funny? Now and zen...Oh, Christ! Who writes this shit?

**Did you hear the one about the Zen Buddhist who called to order a pizza?**
He said, "Make me one with everything."

The pizza delivery man hands the Buddhist the pizza and he pays with a $20 bill. The delivery man starts to walk away when the Buddhist stops him and asks for his change.

*The delivery man replies, "Change comes from within."*

**Why can't Buddha vacuum under the sofa?**
Because he has no attachments.

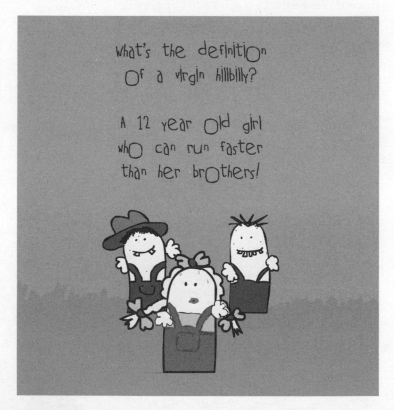

# White Trash, Thugs and Tramps

So, does anybody here admit to being white trash? If you're living in a trailer park, stroking a shotgun and reading this book, you might just qualify. Actually, if you're white and reading this book, I'd think real long and hard.

**What do you call a white man dancing?**
A seizure.

**What is the white-trash boy next door getting for Christmas?**
Your bike.

**What do you call a thug in a suit?**
The accused.

**Two thugs are in a car without any music. Who's driving?**
The police.

**What do you call a kitchen knife in Compton?**
Exhibit A.

**What do you call white trash in a tastefully decorated house?**

A burglar.

**What do Jersey girls use as protection during sex?**

Bus shelters.

# Chinese

The basic Chinese joke for beginners: Ls sound like Rs. More advanced practitioners might like to use their fingers to stretch their eyes diagonally. Yep, you are that low.

**What do you call a Chinese child molester?**

Fuckum Yung.

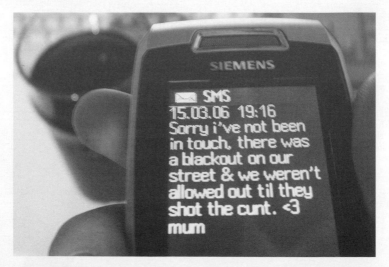

# Blacks

When we started putting this book together people said, "You aren't racists, surely you're not going to print black jokes." Well, if we're going to use spaz jokes, Jew jokes and gay jokes, then it would be unfair to leave the blacks behind. That, my friend, would really be racist.

**What's the difference between a black man and a bicycle?**

A bicycle doesn't sing when you put chains on it.

**Why don't black people dream?**

The last one who had a dream got shot.

**What would Martin Luther King Jr. be if he were white?**

Alive.

**What do you call a black man flying a plane?**

A pilot, you racist.

**Have you heard about Evel Knievel's latest stunt?**

Riding through Ethiopia with a pork pie on his head.

**Two black women with babies are waiting at a bus stop.**

*One says, "Is yours teething yet?"*

*The other one says, "Yes, he's managed to get two car stereos and a handbag."*

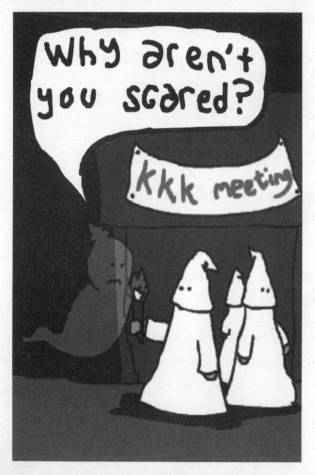

# Irish

On b3ta.com, we once ran a competition called "If Advertisements Told the Truth." Best entry? "Guinness. It makes you fat and turns your shit black."

**What happened to the Irish terrorist who tried to blow up a bus?**
He burned his mouth on the exhaust pipe.

**How do you get a one-armed Irishman out of a tree?**
Wave.

**Why wasn't Jesus born in Ireland?**
Because they couldn't find three wise men or a virgin.

**What did the Irishman call his pet zebra?**
Spot.

**What's the difference between an Irish wedding and an Irish funeral?**
One less drunk.

**Why did the Irishman wear two condoms?**
To be sure, to be sure.

**How do you sink an Irish submarine?**
Knock on the hatch.

**How do you get an Irishman on the roof?**
Tell him drinks are on the house.

**Two Irishmen are sitting on the ground. One falls off.**

**How do you stop an Irish tank?**
Kill the fuckers pushing it.

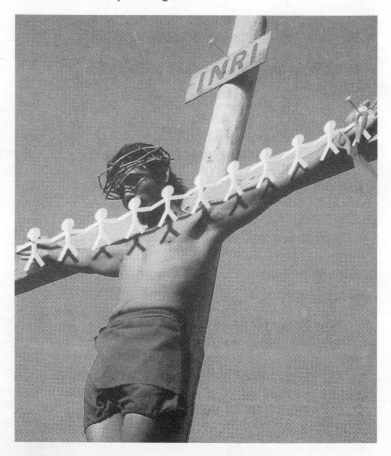

# Illness and Mortality

As you get older, you realize that there is nothing more important to your happiness than your health....Well, that and cigarettes and alcohol.

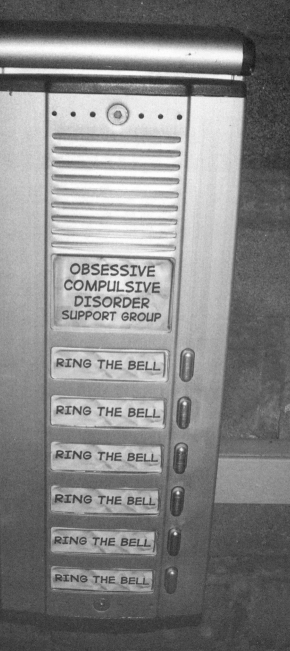

# Disability

Have we offended everyone yet? Who have we left out? We definitely like to consider ourselves equal-opportunity offenders and shudder at the idea that some sorry sap pouring over each joke is feeling neglected right now. So, you know, drop us a line if you're in special need of some light, extremely un-PC humor at your expense. We love charity.

**How did the quadriplegic fall off the cliff?**
He was pushed.

**They say whatever doesn't kill you makes you stronger. Try telling that to someone with muscular dystrophy.**

**What did the mongoloid say to his dog?**
"Down, Syndrome!"

**What's funnier than a drunken clown?**
A drunken clown with Down syndrome.

**What's the best way to fuck a paraplegic?**
Slash his tires.

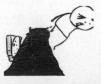

**What's the worst thing about getting a lung transplant?**

Coughing up someone else's phlegm.

*Dyslexic #1: Can you smell gas?*
*Dyslexic #2: I can't even smell my own name!*

**What sits at the end of your bed and takes the piss?**

A kidney dialysis machine.

# A man gets a phone call from the hospital saying that his wife was in a car accident.

**He arrives and the doctor pulls him into a quiet office.**

*"I'm sorry to tell you your wife was in an accident," the doctor says. The man sits down.*

*"She has a broken back," the doctor continues. The man's eyes start to well up.*

*"She will be unable to walk again." Tears start.*

*"You'll have to spoon feed her." More tears.*

*"You'll need to diaper her because she won't be able to go to the bathroom on her own." Even more tears and a small sob.*

*"You'll have to roll her over every two hours because of bed sores." More sobs, floods of tears.*

*"You'll have to bathe her yourself." Starts to slump on the floor.*

*"She'll constantly shit and piss herself." On the floor crying, sobbing and a quietly wailing..*

*"You'll have to communicate for her because she won't be able to." Wailing out loud.*

*The doctor leans over and gently touches the man's shoulder and says, "Relax, relax, I'm just kidding with you...She's dead."*

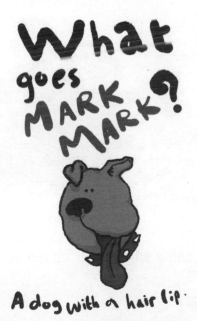

What goes MARK MARK?

A dog with a hair lip.

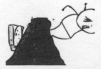

A spastic goes to an ice cream truck. The ice cream man asks him what flavor he'd like. "Doesn't matter," he says "I'm just going to drop the fucker anyway."

How do you know when the vegetables are boiled?
The wheelchairs float to the top.

What's the hardest part of the vegetable to eat?
The wheelchair.

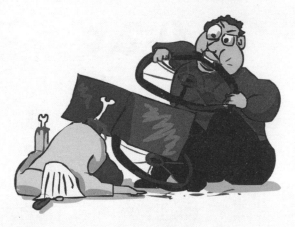

What do you call a wheelchair on top of a wheelchair?
A vegetable rack.

**What's better than winning a gold medal at the Paralympics?**
Having legs.

**How many kids with ADHD does it take to screw in a light bulb?**
Wanna go ride bikes?

**Two dyslexics walk into a bra.**

**What do you call an epileptic in a vegetable patch?**
A seizure salad.

**What do you do if someone has a fit in the bathtub?**
Throw your laundry in quickly.
(Okay, it's not funny. My grandfather died like that. Choked on a sock.)

**How do you get a leper out of the bathtub?**
With a sieve.

**What's a leper's favorite cereal?**
Flakes.

**Why did the leper fail his driving test?**
He left his foot on the pedal.

**What did the leper say to the prostitute?**
Keep the tip.

# Blind

We once went to a fancy restaurant where they served food in the pitch-black dark. The meal was shit, but the experience was awesome. You should try it sometime.

**Why can't Ray Charles drive?**
Because he's blind. (Well, dead actually.)

**What's white and sticky?**
A blind man's eyes.

**How do you drive a blind girl crazy?**
Make her read a stucco wall.

## Why don't blind people skydive?
Because it scares the shit out of the dog.

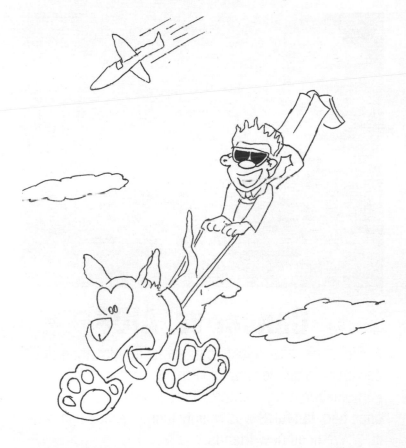

"It's all coming back to me now," said the blind man as he pissed in the wind.

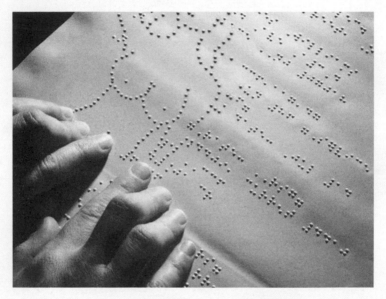

# Cancer vs. AIDS

A friend of ours thinks cancer is funnier than AIDS because science has virtually cured AIDS via combination drug therapy: "It no longer has the sting it once had, but AIDS was mainly funny because gays got it."...We need new friends.

**What's pink, black and has 17 nipples?**
The trash cans behind the breast cancer ward.

**What did the blind, deaf and dumb kid get for Christmas?**

Cancer.

**Why did the little boy cross the road?**

He was on his way to the cancer clinic.

**What can turn a fruit into a vegetable?**

AIDS.

> *Doctor: It's bad news. You have cancer and Alzheimer's.*
>
> *Patient: Oh well, it could be worse—at least I don't have cancer.*

**What are the three best things about Alzheimer's disease?**

1. You make new friends every day.
2. You can laugh at all the old jokes.
3. You make new friends every day.

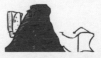

**A woman visits her doctor complaining of a strange feeling in her lower stomach.**

*The doctor examines her and says, "Well, I can tell you that you'll need to be buying lots of diapers in about nine months time."*

*"Am I pregnant?" she asks. "That's wonderful news!"*

*"No, you have bowel cancer."*

# Old People

Here are some jokes to tell your grandpa—assuming you've got one. We don't want to offend anyone by bringing up the death of a favorite relative or anything. We're sensitive souls, you see.

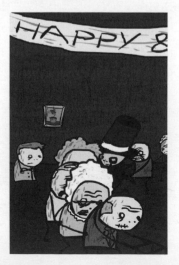

**What's 100 yards long and smells like piss?**
The post office line on Thursday mornings.

**What's blue and fucks old ladies?**
Hypothermia.

**What's red and fucks old ladies?**
Republicans.

**What's got 100 balls and fucks old ladies?**
Bingo.

**What's blue and fucks grannies?**
Me in my lucky blue coat.

**Little Billy is sucking his grandma's tit and some white stuff spurts into his mouth. "Hey, Grandma," says little Billy, "aren't you a little old to be producing milk?"**

*"Aw, Billy," says his doting grandmother, "that isn't milk, it's cancer."*

**How do you get a granny to shout "Cunt!"?**
Get another one to shout "Bingo!"

**What's pink and smells like ginger?**
Fred Astaire's fingers.

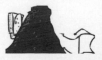

**How do you make a granny's toes curl?**
Fuck her with her tights on.

**What's pink and wrinkly and hangs out of your grandad's underpants?**
Your grandma.

# Dead Babies

We have a theory on dead baby jokes: They're for young kids who know that their moms wouldn't approve. However, if you become a parent yourself, they stop being funny.

**What's black and does your child's hair for you?**
Leukemia.

**What's bright red-pink, 18 inches long and makes women scream?**
A parrot eating a baby.

**What is red and bubbly and goes around banging on windows?**
A baby in a microwave.

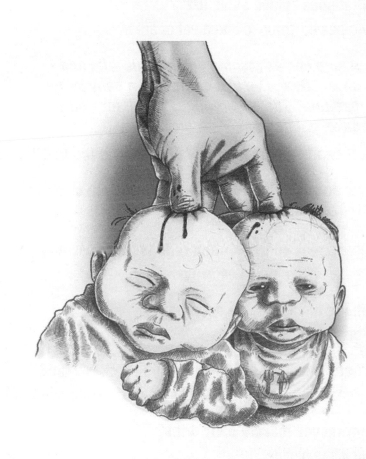

**What goes "plink, plink, fizz"?**
Two babies dropped into a vat of acid.

*A man comes rushing down to his wife and says, "Dear, I've just dropped the baby in the bathtub." The wife replies, "Well, for God's sake, get her out!"*

*"I can't," the man says. "The water's too hot."*

**How do you get a baby to stop crawling in circles?**
Nail its other foot to the ground.

**What's pink and silver and runs around screaming?**
A baby with a fork in each eye.

**What's funnier than a dead baby?**
A dead baby in a clown suit.

**What's funnier than a dead baby in a clown suit?**
A dead baby in clown suit sitting next to a retarded kid.

**How do you make a baby drink?**
Put it in a blender.

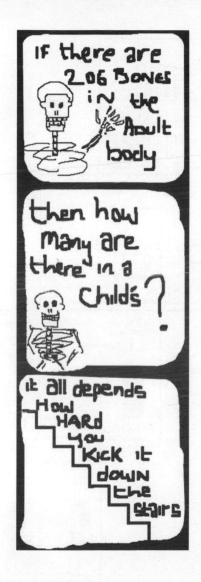

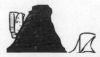

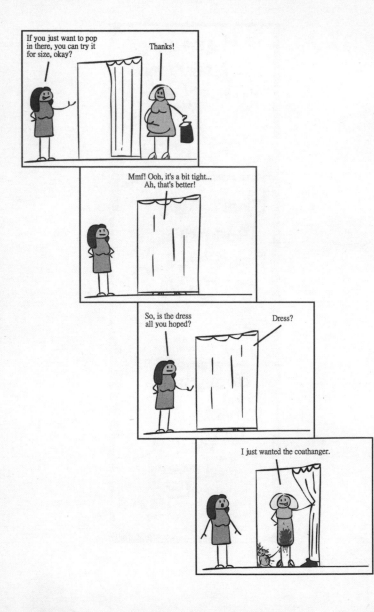

**What's the worst thing about drinking a newborn-baby smoothie?**

The sound the mother makes watching you make it.

**What's red and has an arm and four legs?**

A pit bull in kindergarten.

**What's worse than a truck full of dead babies?**

A truck full of dead babies with one live baby in the middle eating its way out.

**What's one foot high, pink and dancing?**

A baby on a barbecue.

**Why did the baby fall out of the tree?**

It was dead.

**What's worse than ten babies in a cramped crib?**

One baby in ten cribs.

**What's red, slimy and crawls up a woman's leg?**

A homesick abortion.

**How do you get 100 babies in a bucket?**
With a blender.

**And how do you get them back out?**
Doritos!

**What do you call two abortions in a bucket?**
Blood brothers.

**How many babies does it take to paint a wall?**
Depends how hard you throw them.

**What sits quietly in the corner and gets smaller and smaller?**
A baby with a cheese grater.

**What's red and pink and sits in the corner with its smile getting bigger and bigger?**
A baby eating razorblades.

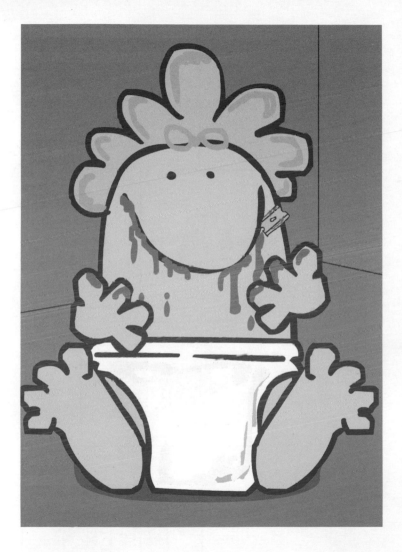

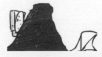

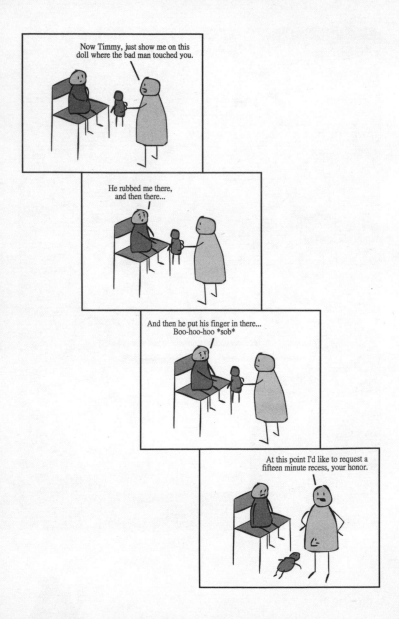

**What's purple, covered in pus and squealing?**
A peeled baby in a bag of salt.

**How do you make a dead baby float?**
Add Coca-Cola and two scoops of ice cream.

**What's blue, purple, pink and sits in the corner?**
A baby with an elastic band around its neck.

**What is 12 inches long, pink and stiff, and makes women scream all night long?**
Crib death.

**What's black and blue and smokes in the corner?**
A baby chewing on an extension cord.

**What's white, round and fucks small children?**
Aspirin.

**What's blue and orange and lies at the bottom of a swimming pool?**
A baby with burst floaties.

**Hear about the back-alley abortionist whose business folded?**
His ferret died.

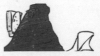

**What's the difference between a train carriage and miscarriage?**

You can't eat a train carriage.

**What's the difference between a Ferrari and a pile of dead babies?**

I don't have a Ferrari in my garage.

**What's the difference between a truck load of babies and a truck load of marbles?**

You can't pitchfork marbles.

**What's the difference between a dead baby and an apple?**

I don't come all over an apple before eating it.

**What's the difference between a dead baby and a rock?**

You can't fuck a rock.

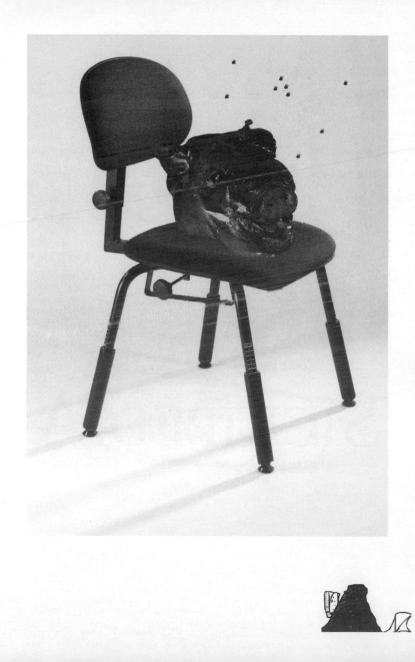

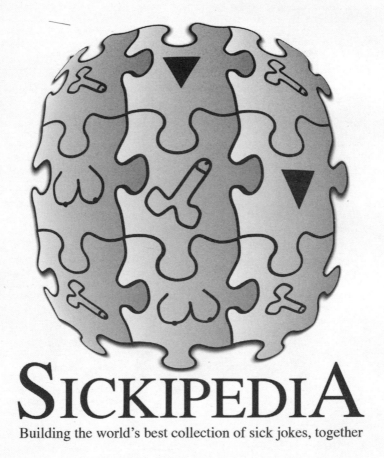

# SICKIPEDIA

Building the world's best collection of sick jokes, together

# Jokes with no home

•   •   •

Not all jokes have somewhere to live. Maybe you'll take these under your tender wing?

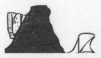

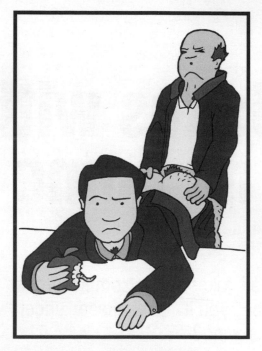

**What's worse than finding half a worm in your apple?**

Rape.

**What's the difference between snot and cauliflower?**

Kids will eat snot.

**What smells worse than the smell of a dead anchovy?**

A dead anchovy's cunt.

# Anti-jokes

Some jokes work by confounding your expectations. Some work by expecting you to know the punch line and going somewhere different. Like these little beauties…

**What's gray and comes in pints?**
My spunk.

**What's yellow and tastes like piss?**
Piss.

**What's brown and sticky?**
A stick.

**What goes in long and hard and comes out soft and sticky?**
Chewing gum.

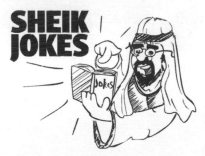

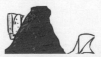

**What did the deaf, dumb and blind kid get for Christmas?**

A pinball machine.

**How do you get a clown off a swing?**

Hit him with an axe.

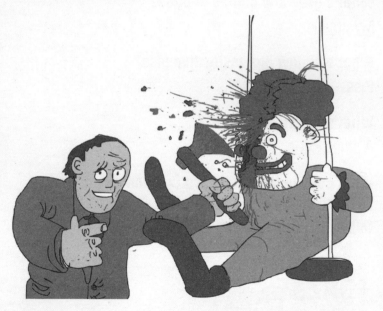

**Knock knock!**

*Who's there?*

**Cancer!**

**Why did the girl fall off the swing?**

Because she had no arms.

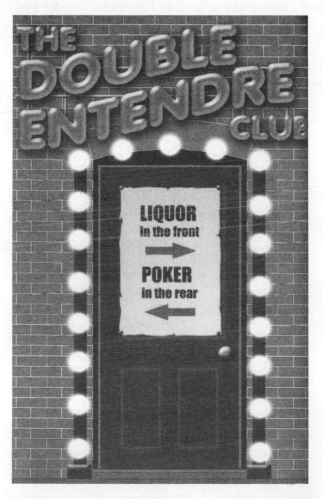

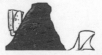

# Police and Hippies

**What animal has a cunt in the middle of its back?**
A police horse.

**What's orange and looks good on a hippie?**
Fire.

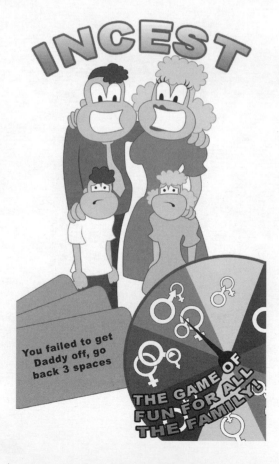

# One-liners

We've concentrated on jokes that are two-liners. Here's others that didn't quite fit but we liked sticking in anyway.

Yes, Mrs. Lincoln, but did you enjoy the play?

Mrs. Kennedy, how was the parade?

I want to die in my sleep like my grandpa, not kicking and screaming like his passengers.

Did you hear about the gynecologist who decorated his house through the mail slot?

It costs $0.10 to send this text message. That's enough for an African child to buy enough food and water to live on for a WHOLE DAY. Send this message to seven people and starve the cunt for a week.

A paraplegic walks into a bar. Only joking...

In today's news, police in Alabama found the body of black man hanging from a tree. His arms and legs had been cut off, and he'd been set on fire and shot seven times. The sheriff said it was the worst suicide he'd ever seen.

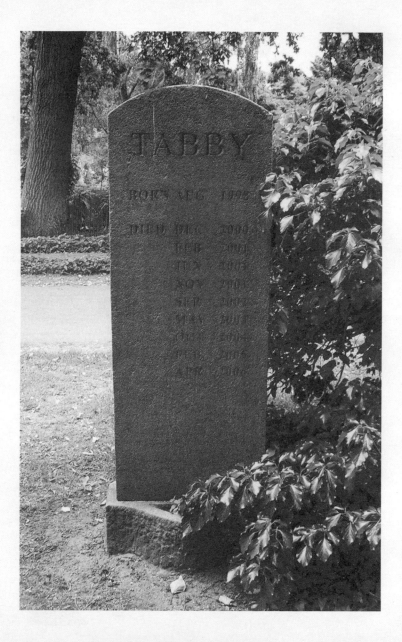

# Cruelty to Animals

There's really nothing funny about cruelty to animals. Except when those animals are vicious, man-eating psychopath killers. Like baby seals. And kittens.

**A baby seal walks into a club...Boom. Boom.**

**How do you stop a dog from humping your leg?**
Suck its cock.

**What's black and white and red all over?**
Panda rape.

**What do you have when your donkey and your rooster get in a fight, and the donkey bites the rooster's leg off?**
A foot of cock up your ass.

**What do you call a dog with no legs?**
Anything you want, it still won't fucking come to you.

**What's the difference between a cow and a hamster?**
The cow survived branding.

**What's got 100 balls and fucks rabbits?**
A shotgun.

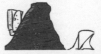

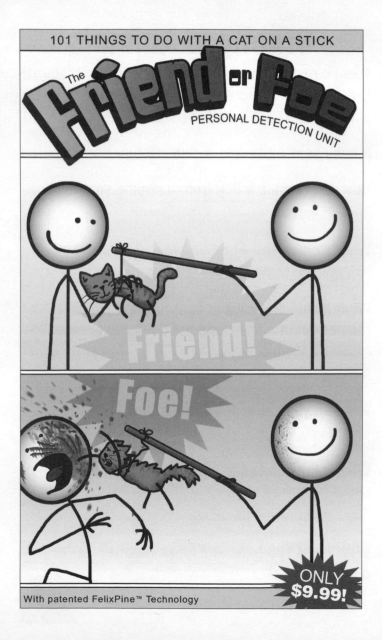

**What do you call a deer with no eyes?**
Bambi's mom.

**Two guys are walking down the street and see a dog on a lawn licking its balls. One guys says to the other, "Man, I sure wish I could do that." The other guy says, "Don't you think you ought to pet him first?"**

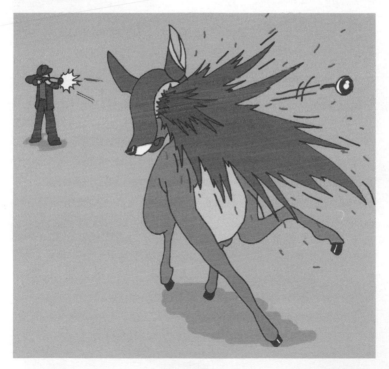

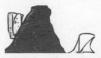

**Why didn't the cat eat its dinner?**
Because its head was nailed to the floor.

**What do you do if a kitten spits at you?**
Turn the griddle down.

**What's yellow and smells like bananas?**
Monkey barf.

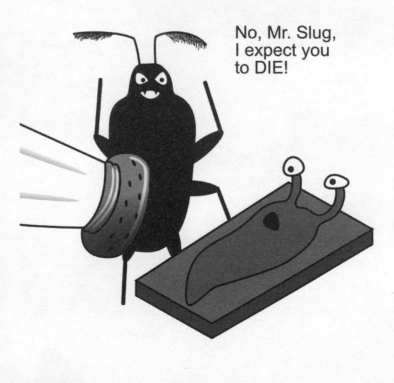

**What's got four legs and goes "meow"?**
A frozen dog on a bench saw.

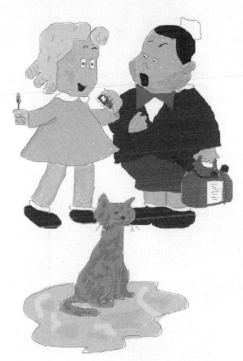

**What's gray and comes in pints?**
An elephant.

**What is green and smells like pork?**
Kermit's fingers.

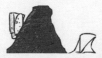

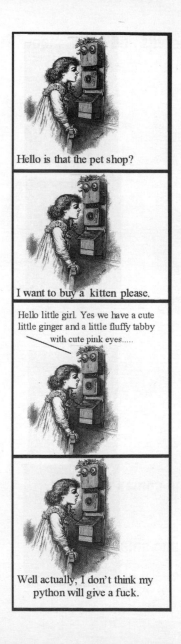

**What do you do if you come across a tiger in the jungle?**
Wipe it off and apologize.

**How do you make a dog go "meeeooowwww"?**
Tie it to a motorcycle.

**What do you do if an elephant comes through the window?**
Swim!

**What do elephants use for tampons?**
Sheep.

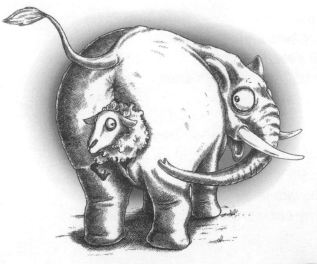

**What's green and red and goes around and around and around?**

Kermit the Frog in a blender.

# Poetry Corner

Really, no respectable joke book lacks a little rhyme and meter. Poetry, after all, is the thinking man's form of a joke.

**Jack and Jill went up the hill**
**So Jack could lick Jill's fanny,**
**All he got was a mouth of cum**
**'Cuz Jill's a fucking tranny.**

Not quite a joke…
**There was an old woman**
**Who lived in a shoe,**
**She had so many children**
**Her cunt fell out.**

**There once was a man from Nantucket**
**Whose dick was so long he could suck it.**
**He said with a grin**
**As he wiped off his chin**
**"If my ear were a cunt, I would fuck it."**

There was a young man named Dave
Who kept a dead whore in a cave
He said, "I admit,
She does smell a bit,
But look at the money I save."

I love my dog and he loves me,
And that's the way love's supposed to be,
But when it comes to having sex,
"Woof woof woof!" barks my dog Rex.

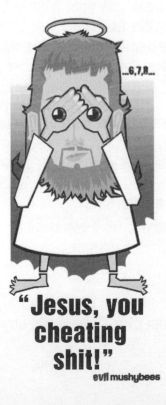

...6,7,8...

"Jesus, you
cheating
shit!"

evil mushybees

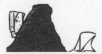

# Mime Jokes

Aha! This part of the book is a little different. These are jokes for you to learn and act out for your friends in the bar. They're our favorites.

**How many shredded wheat does Superman eat for breakfast?**

(Pause, stare at them, and blink twice.)

**You're sitting in a bar. Ask your friends what a woman says after her first blow job. Take a sip of your beer as they ponder the answer, and hold the beer in your mouth. Pause for a few seconds, then say, "I wuv you!" and let the beer spurt everywhere.**

**Why was Jesus so popular with the ladies?**

Because he was hung like THIS. (Assume crucifix position, palms forward as if indicating penis size.)

**How does Jesus masturbate?**

(Stretch your arms out, as if you were on a cross, and make downward grabbing motions with your mouth like you're attempting to suck yourself off. Extra points for miming frustration.)

**What does the cum of a 12-year-old boy smell like?**

(Exhale.)

**What's this?**

(Stick some paper money under your chin and drool.)
Stephen Hawking at a titty bar.

**What's this?**

(Sit at an awkward angle and dribble.)
Stephen Hawking on being told his wife has died.

**What's this?**

(Hold thumb and forefinger a centimeter apart.)
I came this close to a blow job last night.
(Bend over as far as you can and try to reach
your crotch with your mouth.)

**What's this?**

(Assume crucifix position with feet and legs firmly
together, and then swing arms and torso in a bendy,
circular fashion.) Jesus on a rubber cross.

**What's this?**

(Assume crucifix position with feet and legs firmly
together, neck slack in a recently deceased way.)
A shitty way to spend Easter.

**What does a gay man say after sex?**

(Let some frothy spit dribble out your mouth.)

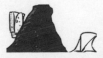

## What's this?

(Rub your chin against each shoulder while grinding your teeth.)
Superman putting on his cape.

## What's this?

(Make wheelchair motion with your hands, but occasionally flick your head back.)
The Paralympic hurdles.

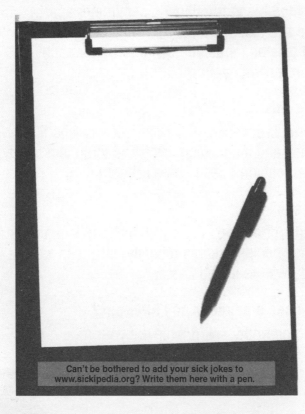

Can't be bothered to add your sick jokes to
www.sickipedia.org? Write them here with a pen.

# Panic Page

• • •

Take a breath. Think of the kittens. Think of the kittens. Take a breath.

Think of the kittens. Take a breath. Think of the kittens. Take a breath.

Think of the kittens. Take a breath. Think of the kittens.

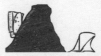

**How do you kill a circus?**
Go for the juggler.

**What's a shitzu?**
A zoo with no animals.

**Why does Edward Woodward have so many Ds in his name?**
Because otherwise he'd be Ewar Woowar.

**Two cows are in a field. One says, "I'm not scared of mad cow disease." The other says, "Oh really, why not?" The first one replies, "Because I'm a helicopter."**

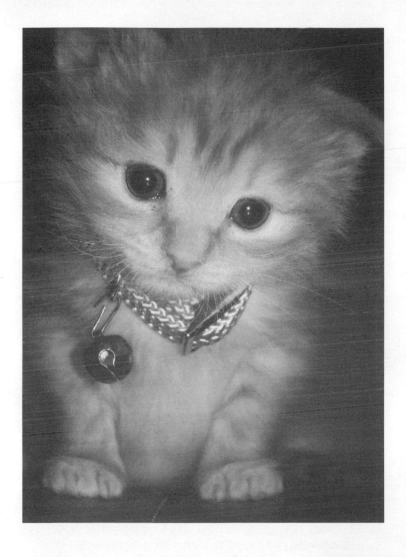

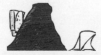

## Thanks to

None of this would be possible without Lucy, David Stevenson, Rob Tinsley, Mike Trinder, Fraser Lewr, Joel Veitch, Denise Wilton, Steven D Wright, Jonathan Blyth, Robert Popper, Cal Henderson, Tomsk and all at B4ta, and Paul and Clare from The Friday Project

## Jokes supplied by

100% Cock, _earwaxuk_, AdrianJ, Albert the Mildly Deranged, alexr, Amazing Mr Strange, animalsinclothes, Arnolfini, asme, assistant commissioner terra blanche, Avast, Axis: Bold as love, Bad Horsey, badbadger, bakelit72, baldmonkey, barronshark, Bearos, Beastie, beatpig, beergut, bennyhillslovechild, Bern, Bertie Dastard, bigbadtone, bilbobarneybobs, Bill Stickers, blindspot, Bob Hopelessness, BorderlineSchizo, boyx, busterbeckett, Butters, Cabus, Caligula, camel-related incident, Cap'n Tallbeard, captain emo, Cashy, caspar_ghodd, CdrVimes, Celebral, chalky_bumface, Charlie Baked Potato, Charlie big bananas, cheesebread, Cheesemonger, Cherry Dude, Chuckman, Citadel, ClockworkDespot, cosmicmuffdivers, craddster, crayongirl, crispyshark, daddyk, dan666, dani_B, Darkpie, Daveh, Daveybaby, DeadCats, Dinsdale v Spiny Norman, Dixon_Bawls, Dizzy Bob loves nuts, djgalaxe, DoctorDeath, Dogmatix, doltage, donkeysoup, Dont point it at your face, Dooley, Durch Den Monsun, DustyD, elgonzorelli, Elsie Charsnal, Eumphazard, Exelcior, fatcatpat, ferret charmer, Fire and Forget, Fishgoth, Flapjack, fox_handybread, fractalpat, fried gold, frogdoctor, Funkwomble, fwack, Gadzooks, Gaz, gedo69, gedo69, geegee, gehenna, gentleben, Ghost rider on a unicycle is on aunicycle, Gibber, gilesmthomas, gizmo, Gizmo.MP3, grandmasterfluffles, grey kid, griffin147, gronkpan, gstewart3000, gumball, HairyBaldy, HairyTwatter, Haku, HappyM, hot wee wee jefferson, Humpty Dumpty was Pushed, i_live_in_a_bubble, I'm new! chocapocalyptic, Insane Maniac, Jam Master Geordie, jeccy, JKF, JLB8, jme, Joel Roddy, johnny chode, JohnPaulCassanova, jo-jo the majic clown, jonnybignose, JonnyMX, JTsteelblu, Kage, kalimah, Kaziko, KernKraft, Kersal Missive, king cnut-works for fcuk, kinks, kiss_my_bunni, Kong, Kuroi Kyo, La Chockita, Lamby, Lanc, Last Night A DJ Battered My Christ, lat297, Laughing Boy, lightie, Lilith, Limpy713, Llamanator, lo, localknowledge, lohr, Lord Monkey of Yorkshire, lordironlung, Loz, Lozhead, m0n|<eY, MadPeeps, maiden, Marn, mcintoish, meatybrain, Mehitabel_Itrang, MeZ, Miharu, mike woz ere, mikek01, Milo the crab, mindlouse, Mischeivious_Delinquent_Squirrel,